When Quitting Isn't an Option

How to survive and grow inside the job you already have

DEDICATION

For my husband, Ryan, for always encouraging me to choose my own path and for listening as I worked through more ideas than I can count.

For my children, Jordan, Sophie, and Collin, who are a constant light in my life.

For my sister, Shena, who reads everything I throw her way and tells me the truth when it matters.

For every boss I've ever had — good and bad — who taught me, in different ways, the kind of leader I wanted to be.

For every employee who worked for me or beside me along the way: I saw you. I learned from you. You shaped how I understand what makes work more human.

This book is a work of nonfiction based on real workplace dynamics. Any
resemblance to actual people, organizations, or events is unintentional and
coincidental. Examples and scenarios have been generalized to protect
privacy.

ISBN: 979-8-218-90095-3

Printed in the United States of America

A Quick Note Before You Start

This book gives you real-world tools, phrases, and ideas you can use at work. Every workplace is different, and every situation comes with its own risks. Please use what fits your role, your company, your industry, and your comfort level.

Nothing in this book is legal advice, HR advice, or a guarantee of specific outcomes. These pages are here to help you feel more confident, clearer, and more in control, not to replace your judgment, your employee handbook, or any laws.

You know your workplace better than anyone.

Take what helps. Leave what doesn't.

Use your voice in a way that keeps you safe and supported.

Table of Contents

Introduction: For Everyone Who's Still Showing Up

So Your Job Feels Like Too Much...1

So You're Efficient (and It's Being Used Against You)...........8

So You're Carrying the Whole Team...15

So You're Stuck With a Micromanager 21

So You're Always Out of the Loop 27

So You Can't Say No 33

So Recognition Never Comes...42

So You Got Passed Over 50

So You're Underpaid and Overdue..57

So You Feel Invisible at Work 64

So the Work Keeps Changing..73

So Your Workplace Is Toxic 82

So You're Ready for What's Next..99

The Employee Survival Toolbox 109

Epilogue...113

About the Author..115

Introduction: For Everyone Who's Still Showing Up

Most of us can't just walk out or start over. The job market is rough, and the bills don't wait. You might not love where you work right now, but you still show up. You're good at what you do, and sometimes that's exactly why it's so hard.

Maybe you've been overlooked, overworked, or just plain tired of doing more than your fair share. You've seen coworkers coast while you carry the weight. You've had bosses who mean well but don't listen. You've given your best ideas to people who barely noticed. And somehow, you're still there just trying to make it work.

This book is for you.

Before You Try Any Strategy in This Book

Remember, nothing here is legal advice or HR guidance. These ideas are designed to help you communicate with confidence and protect your sanity, but you should always adapt them to your environment, workplace policies, and personal safety.

You already know the rules, you're just trying to survive inside them.

This book is not a pep talk about quitting or a promise that if you just "manifest harder," your dream job will appear. It's a **field manual for surviving and succeeding inside the job you already have.**

Sometimes you can't change everything, but you can change *something*.

You can communicate differently.

You can build better boundaries.

You can take back your time, your confidence, and your sense of purpose, even in a place that doesn't always make it easy.

Each chapter in this book starts with a moment you've probably lived through: getting passed over for promotion, dealing with a micromanaging boss, carrying everyone's workload, being left out of decisions, or watching new technology threaten your role.

You'll find practical steps and real scripts you can use right away. Not the kind that will get you fired, but the kind that helps you stay professional, confident, and sane.

Some ideas might not work where you are. That's okay. The goal isn't perfection. It's finding progress you can live with.

Along the way, you'll see small exercises to help you reflect, examples from real workplaces, and simple tools to use in conversations that matter. Toward the end, you'll find career-building sections, like how to update your resume, how to describe your experience in interviews, and how to take what you've learned here to your next step whenever that time comes.

You don't have to wait for a better job to feel better about working. You can start finding your footing right now, right where you are.

How to Use This Book

You can read this book straight through or skip straight to the chapter that fits what you're dealing with right now.

Every chapter stands on its own. Every tool works on its own.

Workplaces are complicated. Your situation may shift from week to week. Come back to the parts you need, when you need them. There's no wrong order here, just support for whatever you're carrying today.

As you read, you may recognize yourself in more than one chapter. That's not a sign you're doing something wrong. Workplace patterns rarely show up one at a time. Overload often leads to invisibility. Efficiency gets punished, which leads to burnout. Poor communication feeds micromanagement. Toxicity doesn't arrive all at once; it builds as small issues go unaddressed.

If several chapters feel familiar, it doesn't mean you're the problem. It means the pressure has been stacking. This book isn't meant to diagnose you or your workplace, it's meant to help you recognize patterns clearly so you can respond with intention instead of self-blame.

There's no wrong place to begin. Start with what feels most familiar.

Chapter 1

So Your Job Feels Like Too Much

How to stay afloat when the workload never ends, and how to speak up without sounding like you're complaining.

Most of us have lived this scene: you start the day with a plan. You know what you need to finish, what you can handle, and maybe, if nothing goes wrong, you'll clock out on time. Then your boss stops by with *one quick task*. Someone calls in sick. A customer needs help. An email pings that can't wait. By mid-afternoon, you've handled ten surprises and finished none of the things that actually mattered. You drive home with a full day behind you and almost nothing to show for it.

Jobs can start to feel too heavy for different reasons. Maybe the workload keeps growing no matter how much you do. Maybe the rules or goals keep shifting, and you can't tell what matters anymore. Or maybe life outside of work is already hard, and the job just adds weight you don't have room for. Whatever the reason, feeling stretched doesn't mean you're weak. It means you're human.

When the Work Keeps Multiplying

If you're dependable, quick, or the person who "just gets it done," people learn to lean on you. Extra shifts, extra projects, extra everything. At first, it feels good, proof that you're trusted, but slowly it becomes the reason you never catch up.

In a coffee shop, that might look like covering the register *and* drive-through because you're the only one who can handle the rush without melting down. In an office, it's being handed every "urgent" report because you'll turn it faster than anyone else. On a crew site, it's finishing your section early only to get sent to help everyone else finish theirs.

Dependability turns invisible; all they see is capacity. Being good at your job can quietly turn into being expected to absorb more than your role was built to hold.

That's when it helps to name the limit out loud.

When you're asked to stay late after already carrying a full day:
"I can stay late tonight if we really need coverage, but then I'll need tomorrow's shift shortened."

When a new task is added without acknowledging your existing workload:
"Here's everything already on my list. What should I pause to make this happen?"

When the workload has real safety or quality limits:
"I can safely handle two more patients; after that, care will be delayed for everyone."

The goal isn't to refuse. It's to re-establish scale. When you make workload visible, you remind people that efficiency has edges.

When the Rules Keep Shifting

Sometimes the job feels impossible because the ground keeps moving. New systems, new procedures, new leadership, new priorities; enough change to make even simple tasks feel unstable.

I once worked under a manager who changed the rules so often that none of us knew where we stood. One week, I was trusted to run the place, and the next, I wasn't allowed to make basic decisions. The work itself wasn't overwhelming, but the whiplash was.

That kind of chaos shows up everywhere. A warehouse worker might get three different packing instructions in one week. A customer-service rep may find their script rewritten overnight with no explanation. A software team might spend months building something, only for management to pivot directions after a meeting they weren't invited to.

It's not the change itself that drains people; it's never knowing what version of the job you're doing today.

When rules, processes, or priorities change constantly, stability has to start somewhere. If leadership doesn't provide it, you're allowed to create your own anchor points so you're not working in a permanent state of guesswork.

When a process changes without warning:
"Before I change how we log shipments, can you confirm this version is final?"

When updates roll out inconsistently:
"Could we update the shared script when edits go live? It would help us stay consistent."

When something new is introduced quickly:
"Let's review this workflow after the first week and see what's actually helping."

When expectations change often, your job becomes protecting your footing. Keep notes. Document changes. Choose one clear focus for each day instead of chasing every shifting demand.

That isn't resistance. It's survival.

When Life Outside Is Already Heavy

Sometimes, nothing at work has changed; you have. Life outside becomes heavier, and suddenly the same job takes twice the energy.

I knew someone who showed up every day carrying more than anyone could see. She was caring for her father after surgery, juggling school pickups, and trying to stretch one paycheck across too many bills. She walked in exhausted, long before the shift even began. The job wasn't the whole weight, it was just the part she couldn't set down.

You don't have to be in her exact situation to feel that.

In healthcare, it might mean holding tears between patient rooms because your own family member is in one down the hall. In retail, it's smiling at customers while wondering if childcare will fall through again. In an office, it's pretending to focus while your phone buzzes with doctor updates or financial worries.

You don't have to pretend it isn't affecting you.

A little honesty can keep things from cracking later. Try one of these:

When you need to explain a dip in energy without oversharing:
"I'm handling some things outside of work right now. If I seem quieter, I'm still focused, just pacing myself."

When you need temporary relief, not special treatment:
"I'll need a lighter schedule for a few days; after that, I can pick up extra shifts."

When you need flexibility to stay functional:
"Could we adjust my schedule a bit this week so I can manage things at home without falling behind here?"

You're not asking for sympathy. You're creating space to stay functional. There's a difference.

When overwhelm is already in the room and you need to slow the pace without shutting down the conversation:

- "What would you like me to pause so I can take this on?"
- "Can we check priorities before I add this to the list?"
- "I'm at capacity right now. Can we look at timelines together?"

Reflect & Reset

Which version of "too much" hits you most often: the ever-growing workload, shifting rules, or heavy life outside of work?

What would *enough* look like for you this week?

What one small conversation could make tomorrow easier?

Write your answers somewhere private. Naming what's real is often the first form of relief.

Quick Win - Try This Today

Before you leave, list three things you actually accomplished. They can be small: helping a customer, keeping calm under pressure, finishing that one form.

This isn't about productivity. You're retraining your brain to see progress instead of pressure.

When It Doesn't Work

Sometimes you'll say all the right things, and they'll still keep piling it on. You'll show your list, ask for priorities, and get another "urgent" task anyway. When that happens, stop fighting for fairness in the moment and protect your energy instead.

Take your full lunch break. Step outside. Walk to your car and sit in silence for five minutes. You can't control what they give you, but you can control what you give back to yourself.

Those pauses are not laziness; they're maintenance. They remind you that you still have power, even when the system around you doesn't work the way it should.

Reality Check

You might not be able to change the system, but you *can* change how much of yourself it takes from you. Boundaries aren't rebellion, they're how you stay strong enough to keep showing up.

Every time you clarify, pause, or ask for order, you remind the world that doing your job well shouldn't mean disappearing under it.

Occasional busy periods are normal. Constant overload without relief is not. Good work should build you up, not break you down.

Chapter 2

So You're Efficient (and It's Being Used Against You)

Turning efficiency from a punishment into a strength, and making your boundaries clear without tanking your reputation.

Most efficient people learn early that being fast, focused, or organized doesn't always lead to the recognition they hoped for. You finish your work in half the time, and instead of appreciation, you're handed more work, more tasks, more responsibility, and more "quick favors." At first, it feels flattering; you're trusted, capable, and reliable. But slowly that trust becomes expectation, and the expectation becomes pressure. You produce more than anyone else, yet your output is treated like proof that you can handle even more.

I once worked so efficiently that my boss actually asked, "What do you even do around here?" He found out the day I left.

Here's the part people rarely say out loud:

- Being efficient gets you more work.
- Being helpful gets you more work.
- Being dependable gets you more work.
- Being invisible gets you more work.

These are all the same emotional injury wearing different coats. Efficiency stops being a strength when the people around you treat it like free labor.

You don't want to complain or seem dramatic. You don't want to be labeled "difficult." You don't want to look ungrateful. You keep taking on more until your value feels like a trap instead of a trait. If this feels familiar, you're not imagining things; you're experiencing a common and exhausting workplace pattern.

The good news is that there are ways through it that do not require quitting, self-sacrifice, or becoming someone you're not.

When Efficiency Gets Turned Against You

There are three big reasons efficient people get overloaded, and none of them have anything to do with weakness or "bad boundaries." It usually comes down to one of these: the work you do is hard to see, your speed becomes the new expectation, or the extra output never comes with extra support. When efficiency is misunderstood or mismanaged this way, even the strongest employees eventually feel stretched thin.

The first is the visibility gap. When you work quickly and cleanly, the process looks easy because you make it look easy. People forget that your speed comes from skill, experience, and the ability to stay focused under pressure. They see the result, not the work that created it. In a restaurant, that might be the server who can handle three sections without falling behind. In healthcare, it's the tech who charts accurately and manages twice the patient load. In an office, it's the person who clears the inbox by 10 a.m. and then gets the department backlog handed to them. Efficiency hides the labor unless you make the labor visible.

The second reason is the comparison trap. Managers start comparing what you *can* do to what others can't, and suddenly, your output becomes the new baseline. Your normal becomes their expectation. Finishing early means you can take on more. Being fast means you should handle what others cannot. Being reliable means you won't say no. You never set this bar; you're just the one held to it.

The third reason is the compensation mismatch. When you consistently produce more, it rarely comes with more pay, more status, or more flexibility. Instead, it comes with more tasks, more stress, and more "can you just…" moments. If jobs paid by output instead of by hour or title, efficient people would be the highest earners in the workplace. Most workplaces simply absorb their productivity without acknowledging the skill behind it.

A Story You May Recognize

Take your average office worker who has been in the job long enough to cut through the red tape and keep things moving. She knows the systems, understands the shortcuts, and can finish a four-hour task in one because she has learned how to work smarter. She organizes better than her supervisor. She anticipates what people need before they ask, and as her reputation grows, everything slowly starts to land on her desk.

When coworkers fall behind, she is the one who steps in. When someone calls in sick, she's asked to cover. When customers escalate, she's pulled in to fix it. She becomes the dependable person, the "just one more thing" person, the person everyone knows can handle it even when she shouldn't have to.

At some point, she slows down, not because she cares any less, but because she is carrying far more than her share. Her manager sees the shift and mistakes it for a lack of motivation, when really it is fatigue from doing her work and everyone else's for far too long.

If any part of that sounds familiar, you're not imagining it. You're tired of being rewarded with more work.

Why This Matters

Efficiency becomes a problem when it turns into expectation. The next step isn't "doing less." It's making the load visible again so people can see the difference between your skill and their assumptions.

This is usually where efficient people get stuck. You know the workload isn't balanced, but you don't want to complain, sound dramatic, or damage your reputation by pushing back the wrong way. You keep absorbing more, hoping someone will notice, until the pressure starts to outweigh the pride you once felt in being good at your job.

You may also feel the pull to ask for a title change or a bump in pay, especially if you're carrying more than your share. That feeling is real, and it matters. Those conversations work best when they're planned, not triggered by frustration in the moment. Efficiency needs boundaries before it needs negotiation.

Later in the book, we'll walk through how to ask for what your work is worth. Right now, the priority is making sure you're not drowning before you ever get to that point.

That starts with slowing the moment down and putting structure back into conversations that have quietly turned into assumptions.

Slowing down isn't a failure or a trick; it's how you stop your maximum effort from becoming the job's permanent expectation.

What You Can Say

These phrases aren't about pushing back. They're about making the workload visible before it quietly becomes permanent.

When efficiency becomes expectation, structure becomes your best defense. These phrases redirect responsibility back to where it belongs without sounding confrontational:

When efficiency is treated like unlimited availability:
"I can take this on. What should I shift to tomorrow?"

When new work is added without acknowledging your current workload:
"Before I add anything else, can we review priorities?"

When timelines assume your speed instead of the actual scope of work:
"I can do this, but not at the current timeline."

When your task list keeps growing without relief:
"Here's everything already on my list. What needs to move?"

When urgency keeps landing on you by default:
"I'm at capacity. If this is urgent, I'll need help with coverage."

Each of these responses does the same thing: it separates your ability from the expectation that you can absorb endless work.

Reflect & Reset

Where do you feel the "punishment" most: more tasks, higher expectations, or being treated like the default fixer?

When was the last time you worked at the pace the job actually requires instead of your personal maximum?

What task recently landed on you simply because you are fast?

Write your answers somewhere private. Patterns show up quickly once you start noticing them.

Quick Win - Try This Today

Make a simple list at the end of your shift with two headings: "What Was Actually My Job" and "What I Picked Up for Everyone Else."

Keep it brief and honest. You don't have to show it to anyone; this is for you. After a couple of days, you'll see patterns: who relies on you, where the extra weight comes from, and what part of your workload isn't really yours. Once you see it in writing, it becomes much easier to set limits without second-guessing yourself.

When It Doesn't Work

Sometimes, even the clearest communication does not change expectations. When that happens, efficient people need a different strategy: match your output to the job's actual requirements rather than your maximum capability. This is not spite, and it is not slacking. It is sustainability.

If the job expects eight hours of work, stop delivering eight hours of output in three. Pace tasks more evenly through the day. Take your full breaks. Pause between transitions instead of sprinting through them. Work at the steady rate the job actually pays for.

This protects your energy without damaging your professionalism. You do not have to exhaust yourself to prove your worth.

Reality Check

Efficiency is a strength, not a sentence. You should not be everyone's safety net. You should not carry the entire system because others will not. Being good at your job should make you valuable, not endlessly available.

Chapter 3

So You're Carrying the Whole Team

How to handle coworkers who coast, systems that rely on you, and expectations that aren't evenly shared.

There's a particular kind of exhaustion that comes from doing your work and everyone else's. Not because you're the fastest or most efficient person in the room, but because the people around you keep leaving gaps wide enough for you to fall into. You didn't volunteer to be the safety net. You became it when no one else stepped forward.

This kind of overload hits differently. It's not about speed. It's not about talent. It's about imbalance. It's about being surrounded by people who coast, or freeze, or avoid responsibility while you pick up the slack because someone has to. You know that if you don't carry it, the customer suffers, the shift falls apart, or the work stalls out completely.

Eventually, you start to notice how uneven the effort really is. Why no one else seems as stressed. Why you're rushing while others clock out on time. That's usually when it clicks: the problem isn't you. It's the way responsibility has been distributed.

When Carrying Becomes the Default

Carrying the team shows up in different ways, depending on the environment. In retail, it's the coworker who disappears during a rush because they know you'll keep the line moving. In healthcare, it's the teammate who takes the easier tasks and leaves you running from room to room. In office jobs, it's the person who always "forgets" deadlines because they know someone else, usually you, will step in before the project falls apart.

Sometimes the issue isn't the people; it's the system. Broken processes. Unclear ownership. Workloads that make sense on paper but never in practice. Your ability to adapt quietly becomes the solution to everything management didn't fully plan for.

Sometimes the issue is leadership avoidance. A manager who doesn't hold people accountable quietly shifts the weight to whoever performs well. Responsibility rolls downhill until it gathers at the feet of the most competent person available. That person is often you.

The pattern is predictable. The more you carry, the more you're expected to carry.

A Story You May Recognize

Imagine someone working in a busy department where no one does their job with the same level of commitment. One coworker disappears for long stretches. Another avoids anything complicated. Another always has a reason they "can't get to it yet." Every shift feels like a group project where only one person cares about the grade.

At first, they try to help. They jump in on the harder tasks, smooth out issues before customers complain, restock items no one else touches, and fix mistakes that should never have happened. They don't do it for recognition.

They do it because they can't stand watching things fall apart.

Over time, something shifts. Others stop stepping in. They start stepping back. The more this person helps, the less anyone else feels the need to. Before long, the entire workflow is built on the quiet assumption that this person will handle whatever gets dropped.

One day, they look around and realize they're no longer supporting the team.

They *are* the team.

If that feels familiar, you're not imagining it. You're exhausted from carrying more than your share.

Why This Matters

Carrying the team is rarely about ability. It's almost always about silence. When you absorb extra work quietly, people assume you can do it indefinitely. They stop seeing the effort. They stop seeing the imbalance. They stop seeing the cost to you.

The first step isn't confrontation. It's making the weight visible so others understand what you've been holding.

You may also start questioning whether the imbalance says something about you, whether you're being taken advantage of, or whether people assume you're fine because you never drop anything. That feeling is real, and there's nothing wrong with noticing it.

This chapter isn't about proving your value or fighting for a new role. This is about restoring fairness so you're not constantly working two jobs while everyone else works one. When the load is uneven, the goal isn't to push harder; it's to stop being the silent solution.

If the imbalance ever starts to feel personal, intentional, or harmful, that's no longer a workload issue. That's a toxic pattern, and we'll talk about those in Chapter 12.

What You Can Say

You don't need confrontation. You need to stop being the default solution.

These phrases help redirect responsibility without creating unnecessary conflict.

When you're already covering multiple responsibilities:
"Here's what I'm already handling today. What should take priority?"

When you're being asked to fix something that needs more than one person:
"I can help, but I can't take this on alone. Who else can support this?"

When helping has quietly become expected:
"I can step in this time, but I won't be able to absorb this on a regular basis."

When your capacity is being ignored:
"I'm at my limit for today. What can we redistribute so nothing gets missed?"

When you're being treated as a replacement instead of support:
"I can assist, but I can't replace someone else's role."

Each of these responses does the same thing: it makes responsibility visible instead of silently absorbing it.

Reflect & Reset

Which part of carrying the team wears you down most: the extra work, the lack of accountability, or the feeling that no one notices?

What tasks do you handle regularly that clearly belong to someone else?

Where could responsibility be handed back without the entire workflow collapsing?

Write your answers somewhere private. Patterns show up quickly once you start naming them.

If you're unsure where to start, look for tasks that would still be assigned even if you were out sick; that's usually where responsibility belongs.

Quick Win - Try This Today

Choose one task today that you normally take on for someone else and simply don't do it.

Not out of spite.

Not to prove a point.

Simply leave the responsibility where it belongs and notice what happens when you let natural consequences do some of the teaching for you.

When It Doesn't Work

Sometimes the weight keeps shifting toward you even after you set limits. When that happens, your strategy has to change.

Stick closely to your actual role. Redirect tasks that aren't yours. Take proper breaks. Complete your own work at a steady pace instead of compensating for everyone else. This isn't laziness. It's allowing the system to experience what you've been buffering so it has a chance to correct itself.

If work quality drops when you stop compensating, that's not a failure on your part. It's information about where the system was relying on you instead of fixing the real problem.

Reality Check

Helping your team is part of being a good employee. Carrying them is not.

You're not meant to be the unofficial supervisor, the quiet fixer, or the person who fills every gap. You deserve support that matches your effort and a workload that matches your role.

Doing more than your share shouldn't be the price you pay for being capable.

Chapter 4

So You're Stuck With a Micromanager

*How to stay confident when someone constantly checks,
questions, or corrects your every move*

There is a very specific kind of stress that comes from working
with someone who doesn't trust you to do the job you were
hired to do. Every decision feels second-guessed. Every task
feels watched. Every small misstep feels magnified. Every bit
of progress feels like it needs approval before it counts.

Micromanagement isn't just annoying, it's draining. It chips
away at your confidence, slows your work, and makes you feel
like you're always on trial. You start to double-check things
you used to know by heart. You feel tense even when you're
doing everything right. You brace for correction before you
finish a sentence.

You're not imagining the weight. It's real.

A Moment You'll Recognize

There is a moment when you realize you're being
micromanaged: you feel someone standing behind you before
you hear them. They're close enough to see your screen, close
enough to comment, close enough that you tense up before
they speak. You weren't confused about the task. You weren't
stuck. You simply weren't doing it the way they would, and
now the air between you is tight with their expectation.

At first, you try to stay patient. You adjust your workflow. You
offer updates. You show your process. The closer they hover,

the smaller you start to feel. Your attention shifts from doing the work to preparing for criticism. You notice yourself hesitating before making decisions you once made with confidence. You're slower, not because you're unsure, but because someone is always watching.

You start to realize the stress isn't coming from the job. It's coming from the person standing over your shoulder.

Why Micromanagement Feels So Heavy

Micromanagement happens for a few reasons, and none of them have anything to do with your ability.

Sometimes it's insecurity. A manager who feels out of their depth over-controls the people around them. In healthcare, that might look like a charge nurse who rechecks every chart because they're afraid of making a mistake. In office jobs, it's the supervisor who rewrites every email because they're terrified of being blamed for sending it wrong.

Sometimes it's a habit. Some leaders were managed this way and simply repeat what they experienced. In food service, it's the manager who hovers behind the line, correcting every small move out of muscle memory, not intention.

Sometimes it's pressure from above. A leader being squeezed by upper management often tightens control on the people below them. The pressure trickles downward whether they intend it or not.

And sometimes, it's simply the wrong person in a leadership role. Not malicious, just unskilled at letting people work independently.

None of this is your fault.

All of it affects you.

Why This Matters

Micromanagement doesn't just slow your work. It changes how you see yourself. When someone constantly checks your decisions, your brain starts to anticipate judgment even when you're alone. Confidence dips. Initiative shrinks. You begin to work from fear instead of skill.

This chapter isn't about confronting your manager or trying to overhaul their behavior. It's about protecting your confidence, communicating clearly, and creating stability in a situation that feels unpredictable.

What You Can Say

You don't need to challenge authority to create breathing room. You just need clarity and agreement on expectations. These phrases stay respectful while reclaiming space:

"I want to make sure I meet expectations. What would a successful version of this look like to you?"

"I can give an update at the halfway point and again at the end. Will that work?"

"Would you prefer progress checks on a schedule, or only when I reach major steps?"

"I can document each step as I go so you can see the full process. Does that help us stay aligned?"

"If something looks off, can you tell me what you would change so I understand your preferences going forward?"

Each one replaces uncertainty with structure.

Handling the Moment They Step In

Micromanagement isn't always planned. Sometimes it shows up in the middle of your work as an interruption, a correction, or a takeover at exactly the wrong moment. These moments feel personal, and responding can take more bravery than people talk about. Speaking up in real time is uncomfortable, but even a calm, simple phrase helps your manager recognize their own behavior and protects your boundaries without creating conflict. What you're doing isn't confrontational; it's steady, professional clarity.

When they interrupt a phone call:
"Could you hold for just a second?"
(to your manager) "Would you like to take this call, or should I finish it?"

When they step into an in-person conversation:
"It looks like you have input here. Would you like to take over, or should I continue?"

When they start correcting an email you're writing:
"I can hand this message over to you if you'd prefer to take it from here. Otherwise, I'll send it once I finish my version."

When they hover while you're completing a task:
"It seems like you may want this done a certain way. Would you like to walk me through your process, or would you like to complete this one?"

When they begin redoing your work mid-task:
"I can hand the rest of this over if you'd prefer to take it."

These responses aren't confrontational. They simply match behavior with responsibility.

Micromanagement thrives when you quietly adjust around someone else's anxiety. These phrases make them choose: take the task or trust you to complete it. Either way, you stop silently absorbing the tension.

Reflect & Reset

Which part of micromanagement drains you most: the hovering, the correcting, or the constant check-ins?

Where do you still feel confident in your work?

What communication pattern would make tomorrow easier: clearer steps, fewer check-ins, or more defined expectations?

Clarity begins with naming what's real.

Quick Win - Try This Today

Choose one task you complete regularly and outline the steps before you begin. Just three or four steps. This gives your manager something concrete to respond to instead of needing to jump in. You're not asking permission. You're shaping the workflow.

When It Doesn't Work

Sometimes micromanagers stay micromanagers. Even with structure and clear communication, the behavior doesn't change. When that happens, your goal becomes protecting your energy rather than changing theirs. Complete your work steadily, avoid unnecessary explanations, document your progress, and create predictability where you can. A micromanager thrives on uncertainty. Consistency helps dial their anxiety down without costing you extra time.

If the behavior ever turns personal, demeaning, or punitive, that moves into toxic territory. We'll talk about those patterns in Chapter 12.

Reality Check

You deserve to be trusted. You deserve to work without feeling watched, doubted, or second-guessed. Being micromanaged doesn't mean you're doing anything wrong. It means someone else can't let go of control. Your job is to stay steady, stay clear, and stay confident, even when someone else struggles to do the same.

Chapter 5

So You're Always Out of the Loop

How to get clarity when information is missing, unclear, or kept out of reach

There's a certain kind of frustration that comes from finding things out last. The schedule changed, and no one told you. A decision was made that affects your work, but you heard it through someone else's group chat. A new process was rolled out, and you learned about it only after you did it the "old" way and got corrected. Everyone else seems to know what's going on, and you're constantly catching up, piecing things together, or hearing things after they already matter.

Being out of the loop doesn't just make the work harder. It makes you question your place on the team. You start to wonder whether you're being overlooked, intentionally excluded, or simply forgotten. You begin to work from a position of uncertainty instead of confidence, and that uncertainty becomes exhausting.

You're not imagining it. Being left out of the information chain creates real stress.

Why Being Out of the Loop Happens

Most of the time, communication gaps aren't personal. They come from messy systems and habits, not intent, but the effect on you is the same.

Sometimes it's the structure.
A workplace has five different ways information is shared:

email, chat, notebooks, shift notes, and word-of-mouth, and none of them are complete. So you end up getting bits and pieces instead of a clear direction.

Sometimes it's a leadership style.
Some managers don't communicate because they assume everyone already knows, or they think certain people "don't need all the details," or they simply aren't organized enough to repeat information consistently.

Sometimes it's scheduling.
Night shifts miss the conversations day shifts have in passing. Part-timers miss important updates because they aren't there when someone "mentions it real quick." Remote employees miss the hallway conversations that never make it into writing.

Sometimes it's gatekeeping.
Someone sits on information because it makes them feel important, or because they are nervous to say the wrong thing, or because they don't want to share decision-making power.

Whatever the cause, you end up paying the price with uncertainty, confusion, and avoidable mistakes.

A Moment You'll Recognize

Picture this: you walk into work and everyone is already talking about a change you didn't know existed. A new policy. A new expectation. A new deadline. They're moving forward, and you're still trying to understand what's happening. You ask a clarifying question and someone says, "Oh, didn't you see the email?" Or the note. Or the chat. Or the meeting you weren't invited to.

You're left feeling behind even though you showed up ready to work. The frustration isn't that you can't handle the change.

The frustration is that no one made sure you had the information to succeed.

If that has happened more than once, you're not imagining the pattern. When information moves without you, performance suffers, and you're the one who gets blamed for it.

Why This Matters

Information is power at work. Knowing what's happening helps you plan your day, manage your energy, and do your job without constantly bracing for the next surprise. When communication is inconsistent, you spend more time catching up than doing the work itself. That's exhausting and demoralizing.

This chapter isn't about demanding perfect communication. It's about getting the clarity you need in a way that protects your confidence and keeps you from scrambling. Being out of the loop often looks like underperformance, even when the real issue is missing information.

What You Can Say

You don't have to call people out to close communication gaps. These phrases help you get the clarity you need while staying professional and grounded, and each one matches the most common reasons people end up out of the loop.

When information is scattered across too many systems:
"Can we centralize updates in one place? It will help me stay consistent."

When leadership forgets to repeat or reinforce key information:
"I want to make sure I'm on the same page. Could you walk me through the main points again so nothing gets missed?"

When your shift or schedule causes you to miss updates:
"I wasn't here when that was shared. Could I get a quick summary so I'm working with the right information?"

When someone is holding information too tightly (without calling it out):
"When you have a moment, could you share the final version with me? I want to make sure I'm doing this correctly."

When you truly have no idea where the update was posted or shared:
"I didn't receive that one. Could you show me where it was posted so I don't miss future updates?"

Each phrase moves the conversation toward clarity without creating conflict. You aren't asking for special treatment. You're asking for the information required to do your job well.

What to Say When You Find Out Too Late

Even when you ask for information, things can still fall through. Here are a few ways to reset calmly in the moment without taking on the blame:

When a change happens you didn't know about:
"I didn't have that update. Can you catch me up so I can adjust?"

When someone assumes you already know something:
"I must have missed that part. What's the current expectation?"

When a process changes without warning:
"Can you walk me through the new steps? I want to make sure I do this the right way."

When someone tells you, 'We talked about that yesterday':
"I wasn't in that conversation. What do I need to know so I can move forward?"

You aren't calling out the gap. You're calmly closing it.

Reflect & Reset

Which communication gaps hit you most: missing updates, unclear expectations, or changes that come without explanation?

Which part of your job feels harder simply because you don't have full information?

What would help you feel prepared at the start of each shift or workday?

Write your answers somewhere private. Patterns show you where clarity matters most.

Quick Win - Try This Today
At the start of your shift or workday, ask one person a simple question:

"Anything I should know before I get started?"

It takes ten seconds and closes the biggest gaps before they open.

When It Doesn't Work

Sometimes communication stays inconsistent, no matter how often you ask. When that happens, shift from chasing information to creating your own system. Keep your own notes. Collect the updates that matter. Confirm expectations before every major task. Build your own clarity where the system fails to provide it.

If communication gaps start to feel intentional, like certain people are always included and others are always excluded, that's a different pattern. We'll talk about that in Chapter 12.

Reality Check

You can do your job well. You can adapt. You can handle change. But you shouldn't have to piece your workday together like a puzzle someone keeps rearranging. Clear information is not special treatment. It's the basic foundation of being able to succeed. You deserve to know what's going on.

Chapter 6

So You Can't Say No

How to say no without guilt, fear, or fallout

Have you ever had any of these thoughts, or typed any of these questions into Google at 2 a.m.?

"How do I say no at work without getting in trouble?"

"Why do I feel guilty saying no?"

"How do I set boundaries without looking lazy?"

"How do I stop volunteering to do everything?"

"How do I say no to my boss without making it awkward?"

If you have, you're not alone.

Being good at your job often comes with a quiet fear: that if you say no, someone will think you aren't committed, helpful, or reliable enough to keep around.

People say, "I can't say no," but what they usually mean is:

"I'm scared."
 "I don't want to look lazy."
 "I don't want to get written up."
 "I want to be seen as a team player."
 "I don't want them to think I'm replaceable."

"I want to be liked."

"I don't know how to say it without sounding rude."

This isn't about weakness.
It's about self-protection.

Workplaces teach people to say yes long before they teach them how to communicate boundaries. This chapter helps you step out of survival mode and back into control of your choices and your voice.

Why Saying No Is So Hard

There are a few reasons saying no feels impossible, and none of them have anything to do with your competence. Most of it comes from the environment you work in.

First, workplaces reward compliance.

From your first job onward, you learn that the people who say yes get treated better. Yes means reliable. Yes means flexible. Yes means promotable, even when it costs you. Over time, yes stops being a choice and turns into a reflex.

You see it everywhere. A retail worker says yes to staying late even though her ride is already waiting. A nurse says yes to taking one more patient even though she's already charting behind. Someone in hospitality says yes to seating one more table, even though it means staying long past closing.

Each yes feels small.
The pattern they create is not.

Second, saying no feels risky.

People aren't afraid of the word no. They're afraid of what comes after it:

A raised eyebrow.
A change in tone.
A comment you can't quite challenge.
The fear of being seen as less valuable.

In unclear workplaces, no feels like a gamble.

A call-center employee says yes to clearing a few more calls even though their break is overdue. A warehouse worker says yes to covering another position because they don't want to be labeled "not a team player." An office worker says yes to a "quick project" even though it means being late picking up their kids.

The request may be small.
The risk doesn't feel small at all.

Third, you don't want to let anyone down.
You care. You take pride in your work. You want the team to succeed. Even when you're overloaded, you worry someone else will suffer if you don't step in.

A front-desk worker covers a lunch even though she hasn't eaten. Someone in tech fixes one more issue after hours. In education and childcare, people stay late because the kids still need help and there's no one else.

Caring is a strength.
It becomes a trap when the system depends on it instead of supporting it.

A Story You'll Recognize

Imagine someone seasoned in the office. He's the person everyone turns to because he always delivers. He remembers details no one else remembers. He notices problems before they start. He picks up pieces without being asked.

One afternoon, his manager stops by with "a tiny favor" due by the end of the day. This person already has two deadlines stacked and a meeting he can't miss, but he hears himself say the word he always says:

"Sure."

He knows he's out of time.
He knows this will spill into his night.
He knows this is the third "tiny favor" this week.

Inside, a familiar script runs through his mind:

"It's faster to just do it."

"It'll look bad if I say no."

"They'll think I'm not helping if I push back."

"Everyone else is busy too."

None of these thoughts are facts. They're learned responses, built over years of being rewarded for stretching himself thin.

Later, he stays late to catch up. His manager thanks him for being "such a team player," unaware that he isn't proud; he's exhausted.

If that sounds familiar, you're not imagining it. Some workplaces rely on the people least likely to push back.

What This Looks Like When It's Working

When this is working, saying no doesn't feel brave or dramatic. It feels calm.

You pause instead of reacting.
You answer with priorities instead of guilt.
Your workload becomes visible again.

You're still helpful, but you're no longer depleted at the end of the day.

If You Skipped Straight to This Chapter...

You're not alone. Many people land here first because this is where everything else quietly falls apart.

If your difficulty saying no comes from:

- **Overwhelm**, Chapter 1 will help
- **Carrying everyone else's work**, Chapter 3 speaks directly to that
- **Someone hovering or controlling your work**, Chapter 4 will help you through it
- **A deeper pattern of burnout**, Chapter 12 addresses that head-on

This chapter is about the moment itself.

The yes you say even when you don't want to.

What You Can Say

These phrases help you protect your time without sounding defensive, rude, or difficult.

Each one fits the real reasons saying no is hard.

When you're afraid of pushback:
"I can take this on, but not with the current timeline. What's the priority?"

When you're already overloaded:
"Here's everything on my list. What should shift to make room for this?"

When the request is reasonable but the timing isn't:
"I can help after I finish this task. When is the latest you need it?"

When helping means doing someone else's work:
"I want to support the team. What part is mine to own, and what stays with the original person?"

When you're breaking the habit of saying yes automatically:
"Let me check my workload and get right back to you."

You're not refusing.

You're slowing the moment down.

A Common Mistake

Many people soften their "no" so much that it disappears.

They over-explain.
They justify instead of clarify.

They say "yes, but…" so often that the boundary never actually forms.

The goal isn't to convince someone you're allowed to say no. It's to state what's realistic and let that be enough.

What to Say When You Find Yourself Saying Yes Anyway

Sometimes the yes comes out before you even realize it. That doesn't mean you're stuck with it.

Here's how to adjust without backtracking awkwardly:

"After looking at my workload, I need to revisit what I took on earlier. Here's what's realistic."

"I want to do a good job on this. I'll need to adjust the deadline to make that possible."

"I said yes quickly, but I need to clarify what I can commit to today."

These aren't excuses.

They're adjustments, and they're allowed.

Reflect & Reset

Think through these questions:

Where does your fear of saying no actually come from: danger, disappointment, or habit?

Who benefits most from your yes, and who pays the cost?

What is one conversation that would immediately lighten your load this week?

Write your answers somewhere private. Patterns are easier to break once you can see them.

Quick Win - Try This Today

Pick one pause phrase to replace your automatic yes:

"Let me check my workload and get back to you."

"I want to help. Let me see what I can realistically take on."

"Before I commit, let me look at my deadlines."

You don't have to say no today. You only have to slow the moment down.

When It Doesn't Work

Even when you communicate clearly, some people push back.

Here's how to stay steady:

When they call it "just a small thing":
"I understand. Here's what I can realistically take on."

When they try to guilt you:
"I want to help, and I'm at capacity. What can wait so I can do this well?"

When they get irritated:
"I'd rather be honest about what's realistic than commit and miss the deadline."

When they ignore the boundary entirely:
Document it, even privately. We go deeper into this dynamic in Chapter 12.

You were hired to do your job well, not to absorb everyone else's.

Reality Check

Your value isn't measured by how much you absorb.

Saying no isn't rebellion or selfishness or disrespect. It's how you protect your ability to keep showing up.

Every time you clarify, pause, or set a limit, you're teaching your workplace something important:

Your time is not free.
Your energy is not endless.
Your yes is earned, not owed.

You can still be dedicated and reliable without being consumed.

Chapter 7

So Recognition Never Comes

How to feel seen when the workplace doesn't notice what you do

Most people don't need constant praise. They just want to know that someone notices they care, that they're trying, that they're doing the work others rely on. But when recognition never comes, something shifts. You start to wonder if any of it matters. You start to wonder if *you* matter.

Maybe the only time you hear your name is when something goes wrong. Maybe you watch other people get praised for work you quietly made possible. Maybe you give your best ideas to someone who takes them to a meeting you weren't invited to. Maybe you do the work but someone else gets the spotlight.

Recognition shouldn't be rare, but many workplaces treat it like a luxury.

This chapter is for the moments when doing your best feels invisible.

Why Recognition Goes Missing

There are a few reasons recognition quietly disappears, and none of them have anything to do with your worth. Most of it comes from how workplaces are structured, not from anything you're doing wrong.

First, recognition systems are inconsistent.
Some managers notice everything. Others notice nothing unless it's on fire. A retail worker may go an entire month without anyone acknowledging the days she held the store together. A hospital tech may keep a department running while leadership praises someone who handled one visible moment. An office worker may solve problems behind the scenes while someone louder receives the credit.

Recognition often goes to the person who talks about their work, not the person who does it.

That's not fair, but it's common.

Second, silence gets mistaken for satisfaction.
When you do your job well without needing help, managers often assume you're fine. They get busy. They get overwhelmed. They forget. They don't realize their lack of acknowledgment lands like a quiet dismissal.

A customer-service rep may resolve a record number of calls in a shift, but because she never complains, her effort blends into the background. A warehouse worker may pick quickly and accurately, yet the only time leadership approaches him is when there's a mistake.

Quiet effort becomes invisible effort.

Third, some roles are built to be unseen.
 Night shift feels this more than anyone. Food gets brought for the day shift. Celebrations happen during daytime hours. Conversations about improvements or changes happen while you're home trying to sleep. You walk in as everyone else walks out.

The result is a quiet, lingering message: *You're here... but you're not really part of the team.*

Behind-the-scenes workers feel it too: cleaning crews, stockers, analysts, support staff. The smoother they do their job, the less anyone notices.

Recognition shouldn't depend on visibility, but too often it does.

A Moment You'll Recognize

Picture someone who cares deeply about their work. She works evenings at a medical office, not quite night shift, but late enough that the building is mostly empty. She handles what others leave behind: late walk-ins, frustrated phone calls, stacks of paperwork marked "later."

One morning, she comes in early for a meeting. The manager praises the day-shift team for "keeping everything moving yesterday." They weren't there for the last four hours. She sits quietly, waiting for her part of the story to appear.

It doesn't.

On her way out, she notices leftover cookies from a celebration held during the day. A note is taped to the box: *Night shift, help yourselves.*

By the time she opens it, all that's left are crumbs.

She didn't need a parade.
She didn't need a speech.
She just needed someone to say, "I see you."

If any part of that feels familiar, you're not imagining it. Being unseen leaves a mark.

Why This Matters

Recognition isn't about ego. It's about meaning. When no one acknowledges your effort:

- Your work starts to feel optional, even when it's essential.
- Your motivation fades, not because you don't care, but because you feel alone.
- Your confidence gets quieter.
- Your ideas shrink.
- Your patience wears thin.

People don't burn out because the work is hard. People burn out because the work is invisible.

You deserve to feel like what you do matters.

Common Mistake: Waiting to Be Noticed

One of the most common mistakes people make here is assuming that being reliable will eventually be seen.

They keep doing the work quietly.
They keep carrying more.
They keep hoping someone will connect the dots.

Most workplaces don't reward quiet contributions, they reward visible contributions.
This doesn't mean you need to self-promote aggressively or become someone you're not. It does mean that visibility sometimes has to be intentional or it won't happen at all.

What You Can Say

You're not asking for special treatment. You're asking for visibility, which is a basic part of being on any team. These phrases help you open the conversation without sounding needy or confrontational.

When your work is invisible because you're consistent:
"Here's what I handled this week. I'd like to make sure you're aware of the results."

When you contribute behind the scenes:
"Since we work opposite schedules, could we set up a weekly update so you have visibility into what I'm handling?"

When you want your work to be recognized accurately:
"I want to make sure credit is going to the right place. Here's what I completed on this project."

When you want more connection with leadership:
"Could we schedule a short check-in each week? It would help me stay aligned and make sure you know what I'm working on."

When you're on night shift, and no one sees what you do:
"Since our schedules don't overlap, could we try a weekly update so we both stay connected to what's happening on each shift?"

These aren't demands, but simply clarifications.

Handling It in Real Time

Recognition gaps often happen suddenly. Here's how to respond without shutting down or sounding defensive.

When someone else gets credit for your work:
"I'm glad the project went well. I handled the reporting portion if you need details."

Or:
"I worked on that piece behind the scenes. I'm happy to walk you through what I contributed."

When a manager says, 'I didn't know you did that':
"I'm glad to clarify. Here's what I cover regularly."

When something you accomplished is overlooked entirely:
"I wanted to share an update on something I finished yesterday. Here's what I completed and where it stands now."

When praise never reaches you:
"I'm glad the project turned out well. I really enjoyed working on my part of it."

These moments are uncomfortable, but they help you stay visible without creating conflict.

Reflect & Reset

Ask yourself:

- What part of my work is the easiest for others to overlook?
- Who actually needs to see what I do and who doesn't?

- What type of recognition matters most to me: acknowledgment, fairness, or inclusion?
- What is one small conversation that would help me feel more connected this week?
- Write your answers somewhere private. Visibility starts with naming what's real.

Quick Win - Try This Today

Send yourself a short end-of-day note:

- "What I accomplished today..."
- "One thing I handled that no one else saw..."

At the end of the week, choose one item to share with your manager or team in a simple update.

You're not bragging.
You're making your work visible.

When It Doesn't Work

Some workplaces simply don't give recognition, not because you're doing anything wrong, but because the culture has learned to function without it.

If you try to be visible and nothing changes, don't shrink yourself to match the culture. Shrinking doesn't protect you. It just makes it easier for others to forget how much you carry.

Here's how to protect yourself in environments that don't acknowledge effort:

- Document your work.
- Build relationships with people who *do* see you.
- Look for recognition in results, not reactions.
- Protect your confidence.
- Remind yourself that lack of praise is not lack of value.

If you begin to notice the culture consistently erases people, not just you, we'll talk about that in Chapter 12.

You deserve to be in a workplace where the effort you give is seen.

Reality Check

You don't need applause to do your job well, but you do deserve acknowledgement. Recognition isn't a reward for perfection. It's a basic sign of respect.

Being unseen doesn't mean you're unworthy. It means the workplace hasn't learned how to see you yet.

Recognition isn't a reward for perfection. It's a sign that your effort isn't being taken for granted.

And you deserve better than crumbs in a box.

Chapter 8

So You Got Passed Over

How to bounce back from disappointment and prepare for what's next

There's a very specific kind of heartbreak that only happens at work. It's quiet, humiliating, and strangely lonely. You aim higher, you prepare, you show up, you put your name in, and then someone else gets chosen. Someone with less experience. Someone with less history. Someone who hasn't done even half of what you've done in that building.

Suddenly, you're standing there trying to keep your face still while your stomach drops.

It doesn't matter how strong you are. Getting passed over hits something deeper than confidence. It shakes your sense of identity.

You start replaying everything:
Was I too honest? Too direct? Not political enough? Should I have tried harder? Was I ever really valued, or was I just useful?

This chapter is for the moment you realize the story you thought you were part of isn't the one your workplace was actually writing.

Why It Happens (And Why It Hurts So Much)

Being passed over isn't one problem, but usually a combination of several. Here are the ones that sting the most.

50

First, they weren't evaluating talent — they were choosing comfort.

People say they want strong leaders, but they often choose the person who feels safest to them, familiar, agreeable, and easy to manage. If you are direct, strategic, experienced, or honest, some interview panels quietly see that as a risk instead of a strength.

They don't say, *"We chose someone who won't challenge us."* They say, *"You just weren't quite the right fit."*

Second, someone less qualified fits a story they already had in mind.

Sometimes the hire has nothing to do with merit.
Sometimes the decision was made long before interviews started.
Sometimes the panel wants someone they can mold, influence, or control.

And yes, sometimes they choose the person who simply makes them feel more comfortable, whether or not they can actually do the job.

Third, your excellence made people underestimate the difficulty of the role.

If you make hard work look easy, people forget how skilled you are.
If you carry teams quietly, they forget how much you've been holding together behind the scenes.
If you solve problems before they explode, leadership may assume the work wasn't that complex.

Dependable people get overlooked because their impact becomes invisible to everyone except the people relying on them.

A Moment You'll Recognize

Imagine someone who built their career step by step, not with shortcuts or favors, but by learning every part of the business. Someone who became the person teams turned to during transitions, new systems, and hard seasons.

When a leadership position opened, people encouraged them to apply. Former coworkers offered recommendations. Their current leader supported them. In the interview, they were steady, honest, prepared. It felt like the moment everything had been leading toward.

Then the call came:

"You didn't move to the second round."

No explanation. No conversation. No chance to show more. Just a door closing.

A week later, they learned who did move forward. Someone with far less experience, someone whose background didn't match the job, someone who had never carried what they had carried.

The shock was instant.
Then came disbelief.
Then the sinking clarity:

Oh. They weren't choosing a leader. They were choosing someone easier to handle.

That moment, that double-hit of rejection and recognition of what happened, is the part that stays with you.

If any of this feels familiar, you're not imagining it. Being passed over is disappointing and disorienting all at the same time.

Why This Matters

Being overlooked impacts more than your résumé. It affects how you see yourself.

When you're passed over, your workload starts to feel meaningless. Your confidence gets quieter. Your ideas shrink. Your motivation fades. Your trust in leadership shifts.

Over time, this kind of disappointment can make you hesitate, second-guess opportunities, and play smaller than you actually are, not because you've lost ability, but because you're trying to avoid being hurt again.

You can recover from this, not by dismissing what happened, but by rebuilding your confidence on solid, honest ground.

What You Can Say

These phrases help you get answers without sounding defensive or desperate. They keep the door open, but they also protect your dignity.

When you want to understand why you weren't chosen:
"Could you share what led to the decision? It will help me understand what to focus on moving forward."

When you want a little more context:
"I appreciate the update. If you're able, I'd like to understand what the interview panel was looking for this time around."

When you want leadership to know you're still interested in growing:
"I'm still interested in future opportunities. I'd appreciate any guidance on what I should work on before the next opening."

When the decision really stung, but you're staying professional:
"I'm disappointed, but I appreciate being considered. I'd like to stay aligned on what growth looks like from here."

You're not asking for reconsideration with these statements. You're gathering the information you need to make your next decision.

Handling the Aftermath in Real Time

When you learn you've been passed over, the entire room feels different. Here's how to handle it without oversharing or shrinking.

When coworkers ask what happened:
"I didn't move forward. I'm taking a little time to think through my next steps."

When people say, 'You should have gotten it!'
"I thought so too, but it didn't land that way. I'm figuring out where to go from here."

When the person who got the job is clearly less qualified:
"It wasn't the outcome I expected, but I hope the role goes well for them."

These aren't about pretending you're okay. They're about staying steady while you decide what comes next.

Reflect & Reset

Ask yourself:

What part of this outcome reflects the workplace, not my worth?
What strengths did I use that still matter, whether they saw them or not?
Who would I be tomorrow if this moment didn't make me doubt myself?

What does this reveal about the leadership I would have been stepping into?

Write what's real, not what you think you "should" feel. You deserve the truth and you can't heal from a story you're still trying to soften.

Quick Win - Try This Today

Write a one-paragraph "leadership snapshot" of yourself:

- your strengths
- the results you've created
- the kind of team member you are
- the kind of leader you aim to be

This isn't for the company. It's for you, so you remember what's still true, even when a decision stings.

When It Doesn't Work

If you try to stay visible, stay prepared, stay open, and the workplace still overlooks you, that's not a reflection of your potential; it's a reflection of their patterns.

Here's how to keep your footing:

- update your résumé quietly
- reconnect with people who value your work
- stop giving away leadership-level labor for free
- watch whether the same people get every opportunity
- pay attention to whether excellence is rewarded or avoided

If the culture repeatedly chooses comfort over competence, your only mistake was ever seeing yourself as the problem.

We'll go deeper into this dynamic in Chapter 12.

Reality Check

Being passed over doesn't mean you weren't good enough. It means the place you're in wasn't ready for you.

Sometimes "no" isn't a dead end. Sometimes it's a redirect. And sometimes, eventually you look back and realize it was the beginning of who you were supposed to become next.

Chapter 9

So You're Underpaid and Overdue

How to start the raise conversation safely, and what to do when the answer is "not now."

There is a moment almost everyone has lived through at least once. You find out someone in your same role is making more. Or a job posting appears for the work you already do, and the salary is higher than yours. Or you take on more responsibility and realize the pay has stayed frozen, even while your workload doubled.

It hits fast. It hits personal. And it hits deep.

Being underpaid is not just about the money. It is about fairness, respect, and being valued. It is about realizing the effort you give is not being matched by the return you receive. When you notice the gap, something inside you shifts. You start replaying everything:

Have I been too loyal?
Too quiet?
Too patient?
Is this really all they see in me?

This chapter helps you face that moment without fear, without guilt, and without questioning your own value.

A Moment You'll Recognize

Picture the person that loved her job. She handled tough customers, trained new hires, covered gaps, and kept the day steady when leadership was scattered. She wasn't loud about it. She just did what needed to be done.

One morning, while scrolling through job postings, she saw it: a listing for her exact role at another company. The pay was almost double. Her stomach flipped.

Later that week, she learned a newer employee had been hired at her own company at a higher rate because "the market changed." No one adjusted her pay when the market changed. No one even mentioned it.

She asked her manager about a raise. They told her to wait until the next review cycle. The review cycle was six months away.

She walked out of the conversation knowing exactly what had happened: the company valued her consistency, but not her worth.

If any part of this feels familiar, you are not imagining it. Underpayment changes the way you carry yourself at work.

How Underpayment Shows Up in Real Life

Sometimes, being underpaid doesn't announce itself. It creeps in through everyday moments you notice.

In retail, you cover multiple roles during understaffed shifts. You run register, stock shelves, and handle customer issues, all at the same pay. Everyone relies on you, but nothing about your paycheck reflects that.

In healthcare, you chart, triage, train new staff, and calm families in crisis. You take on emotional and physical labor no one sees. Raises depend on budgets, not contributions, so you end up doing more for the same amount.

In office roles, you run operations behind the scenes while salaries rise around you. You keep projects organized, anticipate problems, and support everyone else's deadlines. The smoother you work, the more invisible your impact becomes.

These examples look different, but they come from the same story: you are carrying more value than your paycheck reflects.

Why This Hurts More Than the Number on the Paycheck

Underpayment affects more than the budget in your house. It wears on you in ways you don't always notice at first.

You stop volunteering ideas.
You stop offering solutions.
You start watching the room instead of contributing to it.
You feel irritation where pride used to be.
You do your job, but the joy drains out.

The hardest part? You start doubting your instincts. You start wondering if maybe this is just the way it is. You start lowering your expectations so disappointment hurts less.

Underpayment is not just a financial issue. It is an emotional one. And it deserves to be addressed.

Before You Ask: The Responsibility Ladder

A quick reset to help you speak from strength, and not frustration.

Before you start the raise conversation, take five quiet minutes and build three short lists:

What are you responsible for on paper?
What are you actually responsible for in real life?
What results do you consistently produce?

When the lists are complete, compare the first and second list. That is usually where underpayment hides.

This exercise isn't for the company. It is for you. It helps you see exactly what you bring before you walk into the conversation.

What You Can Say

These phrases help you ask for what you deserve without sounding defensive or uncertain.

When you want to open the conversation simply:
"I'd like to talk about my compensation when you have time. I want to make sure my pay reflects the work I'm doing."

When you've taken on responsibilities beyond your title:
"I've taken on several additional tasks over the past few months. I'd like to review whether my pay reflects the scope of my role now."

When you know pay has increased for new hires:
"I've learned the current market rate for this role has shifted. I'd like to talk about adjusting my pay to reflect those changes."

When you want fairness without sounding confrontational:

"I value the work I do here. I'd like to talk about aligning my compensation with my responsibilities."

You're not asking for a favor. You're making a professional request.

Handling It in Real Time

Sometimes the raise conversation doesn't go the way you hoped. Here's how to stay steady.

When they say, "It's not in the budget right now":
"I understand. When can we revisit this conversation?"

When they say, "We'll see at review time":
"I'd like to be evaluated based on my current responsibilities, not just the original job description."

When they say, "Everyone is paid the same":
"I appreciate that. I'd still like to discuss the value and results I bring to the role."

When they try to soften the no:
"I hear you. I'd appreciate a timeline for when adjustments are possible."

You're not pushing back. You're keeping the conversation open.

Reflect & Reset

Ask yourself:

Where is the gap between what I'm paid for and what I actually do?

What evidence do I have of the results I produce?
How long have I been waiting for fairness?
What part of this situation is about the workplace, not my worth?

Write honestly. This moment is not about blame. It is about naming what's true for you.

Quick Win - Try This Today

List three responsibilities you handle that were never in your original job description.
Circle the one that adds the most value to your team.
That item becomes your starting point for the next conversation.

When It Doesn't Work

Sometimes you advocate clearly, calmly, professionally, and nothing changes. That is not a reflection of your value. It is a reflection of the system you are standing in.

Here's how to protect your future when the answer continues to be no:

- update your résumé quietly
- strengthen relationships with people who see your impact
- stop giving away leadership-level labor for free
- watch whether the same people get every opportunity
- notice whether the workplace rewards comfort instead of competence

If you see the same patterns repeat, you didn't fail the system. The system failed to see you clearly.

We will talk more about what that means in Chapter 13.

Reality Check

Being underpaid does not mean you misjudged your worth. It means the workplace misjudged your contribution.

Fairness isn't a luxury. It is a baseline for healthy work, and you are allowed to expect better.

Chapter 10

So You Feel Invisible at Work

How to rebuild your presence when no one seems to notice you

There is a kind of invisibility that doesn't show up in performance reviews or paychecks. It shows up in rooms where people talk around you. In meetings where your ideas drift past the table untouched. In conversations where you speak and someone else picks up the thread as if you never said a word.

You start wondering if you're actually there.

The longer it happens, the stranger it feels. You shrink without meaning to. You sit a little quieter. You second-guess when to speak up. You replay moments after the fact, asking yourself, *Was it me? Or had everyone already locked in on other voices?*

This chapter isn't about being unrecognized for your work. It's about being **unseen as a person**.

It's about feeling like furniture in a place where you used to feel like a contributor.

That does something to you. It makes you question your place, your confidence, your voice. It makes you wonder if maybe you were never meant to take up space in the first place.

You were. **You still are**.

Why This Happens (And Why It's Not Your Fault)

Invisibility at work rarely comes from one moment. It usually forms quietly, through habits and environments that reward volume over value.

Here are the most common reasons people start to fade into the background:

Some workplaces mistake quiet for passive.
If you're thoughtful, steady, or soft-spoken, loud people can unintentionally dominate rooms. Not because they're better, but because the workplace never learned how to listen to anyone else.

You've been interrupted so many times that you stopped trying.
This isn't about confidence. It's conditioning. If every attempt to speak results in someone talking over you, you eventually protect yourself by speaking less.

Your role is essential, but not "front stage."
Support roles, behind-the-scenes work, administrative tasks, night shift, closing shifts, these jobs carry teams, but they often get treated like background music instead of the backbone.

You've learned to minimize yourself to keep the peace.
Maybe it started in a previous job. Maybe it started with one manager. Over time, you adapted to survive, but that survival skill is not serving you anymore.

You're **not** invisible. The environment just stopped paying attention, and attention can be retrained.

A Moment You'll Recognize

Picture someone who comes prepared. He's steady, thoughtful, and pays attention in ways other people don't. Before a meeting, he reviews the agenda, writes down a few ideas, and walks in ready to contribute.

When the discussion opens, he waits for the natural pause, that small window where people breathe between topics. He offers his idea clearly.

But the room keeps moving.

Someone shifts their notes. Someone checks an email. Someone changes the subject. A few people talk over each other as if no one spoke at all.

Ten minutes later, another person says the very thing he said, almost word for word... and suddenly it's *brilliant*.

Heads nod. Someone builds on it. Leadership praises the person who spoke.

He sits still, feeling something tighten in his chest. He wonders whether he was too quiet, too calm, not assertive enough. He starts shrinking in his chair without meaning to. By the end of the meeting, he isn't offering anything; he's just trying to disappear without being noticed.

Walking back to his desk, one thought follows him like a shadow:
If I stopped showing up, would anyone even notice?

If any part of that feels familiar, you are absolutely not imagining it.

Invisibility is real, and it has nothing to do with your value.

Why This Matters

Feeling invisible affects more than your participation; it affects your identity.

When you feel unseen:

- Your ideas shrink.

- Your confidence softens.

- Your presence dims.

- Your contributions feel smaller.

- Your voice gets quieter, even inside your own head.

People don't withdraw because they lack value.
They withdraw because the room keeps telling them they aren't needed in it.

You deserve better than that.

Tools for Rebuilding Your Presence

Wanting to be seen without having to fight for attention is not a flaw; it's a reasonable expectation.

You don't need to change your personality.
You don't need to become louder, bolder, or different.

You just need tools that help you take up space in a way that feels natural to you.

Here are a few you can try:

1. The Presence Anchor

Start meetings with one simple sentence that grounds you in the room:

"I'd like to contribute to the conversation today. I have a few ideas prepared."

or

"I have a point I'd like to add as we get started."

It signals that you're participating.
It resets how the room sees you before the discussion even begins.

2. The Idea Stamp

If your ideas tend to be taken away from you, mark them:

"One thought I'd like to put on the table…"
"An idea I want to make sure we capture…"
"One thing I've been thinking about for this project…"

Stamping your idea claims authorship without force.

3. The Interrupt Reset

When someone talks over you, which happens more to women, introverts, and younger employees, you can calmly reclaim the floor:

"I'm going to finish my thought."
"As I was saying…"

"I'll complete my point, then I'm happy to hear your perspective."

It's not rude. It's setting a boundary.

4. The Visibility Loop

Once a week, send your manager a short summary:

"Here's what I completed this week..."
"Here's the progress I made on..."
"Here's one thing I solved that I want to keep on your radar..."

Not bragging.
Not self-promotion.
Just visibility.

What You Can Say

Here are phrases that help you restore presence without sounding aggressive or apologetic.

When your ideas go unnoticed:
"I want to revisit something I mentioned earlier. Here's why I think it matters."

When you're interrupted:
"I'm going to finish my thought, then I'm all ears."

When someone else repeats your idea:
"I'm glad that idea is landing. That's the direction I mentioned earlier. Here's the next step I'd suggest."

When people make decisions without you:
"I'd like to be included in conversations related to this work. I think my involvement will help things move faster."

You're not asking for a spotlight.
You're asking for basic participation.

Handling It in Real Time

These moments are uncomfortable. Here's how to stay present.

When a meeting moves on without acknowledging your comment:
"I want to come back to a point I raised earlier so we don't lose it."

When people speak about your work as if someone else did it:
"I worked on that piece. I'm happy to walk through what I did."

When people consistently overlook you in group discussions:
"I'd like to add my perspective here before we move to the next item."

Small sentences. Big grounding.

Reflect & Reset

Ask yourself:

Where in the workday do I feel the most invisible?
What part of me have I been holding back to keep the peace?
What kind of presence feels natural to me, not louder, just more honest?
Whose voice do I trust more than my own, and why?

Write honestly. This isn't about becoming someone else. It's about letting yourself show up again.

Quick Win - Try This Today

At your next meeting, use one Presence Anchor:

"I have a point I'd like to contribute as we get started."

Just one sentence. You'll be surprised how the room shifts.

When It Doesn't Work

Some workplaces simply do not hear quiet contributors. Not because you lack value, but because the culture only recognizes noise.

If visibility tools don't shift the dynamics:

- start documenting your contributions
- build relationships with people who genuinely see you
- pay attention to who gets space and who doesn't
- notice whether leadership rewards loudness instead of impact
- ask yourself if the room is capable of changing

If the environment continues to erase you, that's not a personal failure.

It's a sign the culture isn't built to hear people like you, and that's a much bigger problem than anything you're doing.

Reality Check

You were never meant to disappear inside your job. Feeling invisible doesn't mean you lack presence. It means the workplace stopped paying attention.

You don't have to stay small just because the room stayed quiet.

You deserve to take up space and to be seen when you do.

Chapter 11

So the Work Keeps Changing

How to stay grounded, capable, and confident when everything around you shifts

Change is part of every workplace now, no matter what industry you are in. New systems, new procedures, new software, new expectations...sometimes all in the same month.

Just when you get comfortable, the process shifts.
Just when you feel steady, the workflow updates.
Just when you think you finally understand the rules, the rules change.

It's disorienting.

Suddenly, you're asking yourself questions that have nothing to do with your talent:

Why does everyone else look like they're keeping up?
Why can't I remember this the way they explained it in training?
Why does the new system feel harder, not easier?

Before you blame yourself, pause here:

You're learning.
You're adapting.
There's nothing wrong with needing time to get steady again.

This chapter helps you regain your footing, not by pretending change is easy, but by giving you tools to navigate it without losing yourself.

Why This Happens (And Why It's Not Your Fault)

Change at work isn't just about learning something new. It's more about unlearning what used to work, and doing that while still keeping up with your regular responsibilities.

Here are the most common reasons change feels overwhelming:

Training seldom matches real life.

You might have been taught the *ideal* version of a process, not the messy, real-world version full of exceptions and workaround steps.

It's not you, it's the gap between the classroom and reality.

Systems often change faster than support does.

Companies upgrade software, tools, rules, or workflows long before they give people time to absorb them. You're expected to stay productive *and* learn something new at the same time.

The new tools don't replace your workload; they stack on top of it.

You're not learning during free time; you're learning while the work keeps moving.

Your brain can't operate at full speed while relearning everything at once.

People forget this: learning something new is a *full cognitive load*. If you feel slower, scattered, or frustrated, it's because your brain is processing, not failing.

Other people aren't "better," they're just ahead in the learning curve.

Maybe they trained earlier.
Maybe they used a similar system before.
Maybe they simply had more uninterrupted time to learn.

Your pace is not a measure of your intelligence.

How Change Shows Up in Real Life

Every industry feels the strain differently:

In restaurants, a switch to a new digital ordering system can turn an entire shift upside down. The buttons are in new places, the timing feels different, and customers don't see the learning curve they only see the delay. You're expected to learn it during the lunch rush with no space to practice.

In warehouses, updated scanners or inventory systems change the muscle memory of the job overnight. Something that used to take seconds now takes minutes until your hands relearn the motions.

In healthcare offices, new scheduling or charting platforms mean the "ideal version" from training becomes chaos when real patients, exceptions, and emergencies interrupt the process.

A Story You'll Recognize

Take the worker who prided himself on being steady. Reliable. The person people came to when things got confusing. When the company rolled out a new scheduling system, everything changed.

Training was off-site and rushed. The examples didn't seem to match real scenarios. People clicked through the modules just trying to finish them. When he finally used the system with real customers, nothing worked the way it did in training.

He made mistakes.
He second-guessed every step.
He felt slow for the first time in years.

One afternoon, a newer coworker said, "It's not that hard. You just do it like this," and clicked through the process without explaining anything.

He felt something he never expected: embarrassment.

Not because he wasn't capable, but because he was learning in public while everyone else seemed to already know what they were doing.

He went home that night, wondering:

Why is this taking me so long to learn? What happened to me being the person who always figured things out?

If any part of that feels familiar, you are not imagining it.

Moments like this make you question yourself, even when your ability hasn't changed.

Why This Matters

When the work keeps shifting, it affects more than your performance.

You start questioning your instincts.
You start apologizing more.
You start hesitating before tasks that used to be effortless.

You start feeling behind even when you're working twice as hard.

Change is not just operational; it's emotional, and the emotional side needs support too.

How to Stay Steady When Everything Changes

You don't have to master the new system instantly. You just need tools that keep you grounded while you learn.

Here are a few that work:

1. The Real-World Workflow

Write down the steps *as you actually do them.*
Not the steps from training.
Not the ideal version.

The *real* version.

This becomes your personalized guide, and it's always more accurate than the official one.

2. The One-Question Reset

When something feels confusing, ask:

> "Can you walk me through how you do it in real life?"

People always have shortcuts, tips, and a version that actually works.

3. The Ask-Again Rule

You're allowed to ask the same question more than once, especially after you've just learned something new. Learning requires repetition, not perfection the first time.

4. The "Show Me" Request

Instead of guessing, ask someone to demonstrate the exact step:

> "Could you show me the part you click on? I learn it faster when I see it."

This removes guesswork and embarrassment.

Ask AI for Help (Without Fear)

You don't have to know everything. You just need to know how to get help.

AI is becoming part of everyday work, and the people who can use it, even casually, have an advantage.

You can be one of them.

If your workplace doesn't allow AI on the clock, you can still practice at home.

Try asking:

- *"Write a professional email explaining I need clarification on the new process."*
- *"Explain this new software like I'm a beginner."*
- *"Give me a step-by-step checklist for _____."*

- *"Turn these scattered notes into a clean checklist I can follow."*

If you're struggling with a confusing new update, copy the instructions into AI and say: 'Explain this in steps a beginner would understand.'

It's like having a personal tutor on demand.

AI makes you resourceful, and resourceful people are always valuable.

Reflect & Reset

Ask yourself:

- What part of this change is actually hard: the system, the pace, or the pressure?
- Where am I holding unrealistic expectations of myself?
- What strengths from the old way of working still apply to the new one?
- Who seems comfortable asking questions, and what can I learn from them?
- What support would make this transition easier, and how can I request it clearly?

Write your answers honestly. Most frustration with change comes from feeling unprepared, not from being incapable.

Quick Win - Try This Today

Pick one task in the new system and do this:

> *Write down the steps as you actually do them, not the way the training described them.*

Just one task.

It will anchor your confidence immediately, and tomorrow, refining it gets even easier.

When It Doesn't Work

Sometimes you try.
Sometimes you adapt.
Sometimes you practice.

And the system *still* doesn't click.

When that happens:

- ask for the "real workflow" experienced users rely on
- request side-by-side practice time
- document confusing steps, so you're not blamed for errors
- look for unofficial guides teams have created
- slow down to a pace that ensures accuracy
- remember, the learning curve is a shared responsibility

If leadership pushes change without support, clarity, or realistic timelines, that is a workplace pattern, not a personal failing.

Reality Check

You're not behind. You're adjusting.

The work changed faster than anyone could keep up, and you're still showing up, learning, trying, and moving forward.

That is not weakness. That is resilience.

You don't have to master the new world in a day.
You're not failing, you're learning, and your confidence will return the moment the new system feels familiar.

Chapter 12

So Your Workplace Is Toxic

How to protect your well-being when the environment is working against you

Some workplaces drain you quietly. Not all at once, but little by little, moment by moment, in ways that make you question things you used to know about yourself.

You start noticing things. You brace before opening your email. You rehearse conversations in your head before speaking. You shrink your ideas so you don't get targeted. And you watch people disappear, burned out, pushed out, or checked out, quietly wondering if you're next.

Toxicity doesn't always look dramatic. Sometimes it looks like patterns that repeat until you stop trusting yourself. When quitting isn't an option, those patterns don't just affect your day. They affect your confidence, your stability, and your sense of control.

This chapter is here to help you get some of that control back.

Not by fixing the system, because no single employee can do that, but by learning how to stop absorbing the damage the system is creating.

Why Toxic Workplaces Hit So Hard

Toxic environments work the same way stress does. They chip at you slowly. They drain your judgment before they drain your energy, and over time, they make you question whether you're the problem.

You're not.

Toxic workplaces run on cycles. Unclear expectations create overwhelm. Overwhelm makes speaking up feel risky. Fear leads to silence, and that silence allows toxicity to keep growing.

You did not create that cycle, but you are the one living through it.

That's why this chapter focuses on patterns, not personalities. It's here to help you stop internalizing what the environment keeps projecting, and to see what's actually happening so you don't keep blaming yourself.

We'll cover the five patterns employees experience most.

- Manipulation Disguised as Policy
- Control & Power Plays
- Favoritism & Uneven Consequences
- Hostility, Bullying & Public Shaming
- Workload Abuse & Burnout Culture

Each pattern includes:

- how it shows up
- a short story or workplace example
- what you can say
- how to handle the moment in real time
- and what to do when nothing changes

You may recognize yourself in one of these patterns, or in several. You don't need to label everything right now. Noticing is enough.

1. Manipulation Disguised as Policy

Toxic workplaces twist rules into pressure.

They say things like:
"Real team players don't push back."
"You can take PTO... but we'll remember who stepped up."
"We're like a family here," right before asking you to sacrifice personal time.

Or, like one workplace did during the holiday season, they sent a fake "holiday appreciation gift card" email as a phishing test, then wrote people up for clicking it.

Leadership framed it as a security policy, a professional standard, a compliance issue, but the execution wasn't about safety or learning. It was about fear.

That's manipulation disguised as policy.

How It Shows Up

- guilt around PTO
- ever-shifting rules that change depending on who's asking
- pressure disguised as "opportunity"
- retaliation when you set boundaries
- being shamed for human needs (breaks, time off, saying no)

A Moment You'll Recognize

Picture a workplace like a car dealership. The sales floor is mostly men. A few women work the front desk or support roles, spending the entire day surrounded by loud conversations, pressure, and constant visibility.

During a slower part of the afternoon, two of the women step out together to grab coffee. It's not about avoiding work. It's about taking a breath, having a moment of safety, and not being the only woman in the room for hours on end.

When they return, the comments start. Jokes about "girl time." Side remarks about being unprofessional. Questions about where they were and why they left together. No rule was broken, but the message was clear. Connection was being watched.

Similar behavior from others never drew attention. Groups stepped away all the time. That wasn't the issue. The issue was who did it, and what it represented.

That's how manipulation works in subtle environments. It doesn't need a written policy. It relies on unspoken judgment to teach people which forms of support and solidarity are acceptable, and which ones aren't.

Another Moment You'll Recognize

Picture this, a worker requested two days of PTO well in advance. The manager approved it, but the week before, leadership sent a message to the whole team: "We're counting on everyone to show dedication during our busiest season."

Coworkers whispered things like, "I guess we're not supposed to take time off now." The worker started to feel guilty about the days they had already earned, days they needed.

That's what manipulation does. It makes you feel wrong for following the rules.

What You Can Say

When they guilt you for PTO:
"Just confirming that my approved days still stand. Let me know what you need from me before I'm out."

When they shift rules suddenly:
"Can you clarify the updated expectation? I want to make sure I'm aligned."

When they try to pressure you into staying late:
"I can help another day, but I'm not available tonight."

Short. Grounded. No apologies.

Handling It in Real Time

When someone uses "team player" language to guilt you:
"I'm here for the team. I also need to follow the boundaries I've set."

When someone implies consequences without stating them:
"I want to make sure I'm understanding correctly. Is there a specific expectation or consequence I should be aware of?"

When leadership tries to shame you publicly:
"I'm open to feedback, but I'm not comfortable addressing it publicly. Let's follow up one-on-one."

2. Control & Power Plays

Toxic workplaces use control as a culture, not a quirk.

How It Shows Up

- leaders who ignore input but demand compliance
- emotional unpredictability
- withholding information to stay in power
- rules enforced on some people but not others
- surveillance disguised as "support"

A Story You'll Recognize

Think about the worker who followed the rules exactly as written, only to be corrected anyway. Expectations weren't enforced consistently. What mattered wasn't performance, but who was speaking and who was listening. Some people were given flexibility. Others were given warnings.

Over time, the worker realized the rules weren't the point.

Control was.

When standards change based on who's involved, people stop trusting the process and start managing perceptions instead.

What You Can Say

When expectations keep changing:
"I want to complete this correctly. What's the current version you'd like me to follow?"

When someone redoes your work without explanation:
"Could you walk me through the part you updated so I can apply it next time?"

When they withhold information:
"I want to make sure I understand. Can you share the details I need before moving forward?"

Handling It in Real Time

When someone steps in just to take over:
"I can hand this part to you if you'd prefer to lead it."

When they correct something trivial to assert control:
"Does this change the required outcome? If so, I'll make the change."

When they give conflicting instructions:
"Which direction should I prioritize so I don't undo work later?"

3. Favoritism & Uneven Consequences

Nothing poisons morale faster than a workplace where rules and consequences change depending on who's involved.

How It Shows Up

- the same people get the best schedules, bonuses, or opportunities
- mistakes punished for some and excused for others
- promotions that make no sense
- "special rules" for certain employees
- loyalty valued over performance

A Story You'll Recognize

A person applied for a team lead role after years of steady performance. They had seniority. They had experience. They had the metrics to back it up. They had trained new hires, covered gaps, and taken on extra responsibility when the team needed it. This promotion felt like the natural next step.

The role went to someone else. Someone with less experience. Fewer results. But a closer relationship with leadership.

When feedback was finally offered, it wasn't about qualifications or readiness. It was vague. "They're just a better fit." "Leadership connects with them more." "They have the right vibe."

There was nothing to respond to. Nothing to improve. Nothing to work toward.

The person wasn't just disappointed. They felt erased. Not overlooked, but quietly written out of a future they had been working toward for years. From that moment on, effort felt risky instead of rewarding. Motivation turned into second-guessing. Confidence turned into caution.

That's what favoritism does. It doesn't just block opportunity. It teaches people that performance won't protect them, and that the rules change depending on who's standing in the room.

What You Can Say

When promotions seem unfair:
"Could you share what qualifications were prioritized for this role so I can prepare for the next opportunity?"

When consequences aren't consistent:
"Can you walk me through how expectations apply across the team?"

When someone else keeps getting exceptions:
"I want to be clear on what the rest of us are expected to do in situations like this."

This keeps the focus on expectations, not blame, and makes the inconsistency visible without calling anyone out directly.

Handling It in Real Time

When someone is praised for something you handled:
"I actually worked on that. Happy to walk through my piece."

When leadership overlooks your work on purpose:
"I'd like to update you on what I completed this week."

When decisions feel workplace political:
"I'm trying to understand what actually matters when these decisions are made."

4. Hostility, Bullying & Public Shaming

Some workplaces let disrespect hide under the excuse of "that's just how it is around here."

No. That's how toxicity spreads.

How It Shows Up

- sarcasm that cuts instead of jokes
- yelling, belittling, eye-rolling
- public embarrassment
- gossip as a weapon
- blame-shifting and scapegoating

A Story You'll Recognize

During a morning meeting, a manager pulled up an employee's mistake on the screen and said, "Everyone look. Don't ever do this." There was no context. No explanation of what went wrong. No guidance on how it could have been handled differently.

People laughed nervously, the way they do when they don't want to be next. The room moved on, but the moment didn't. The employee barely spoke for the rest of the meeting. Their hands shook. They spent the rest of the day replaying it, wondering who else had noticed, who else was judging, and whether that single mistake would now define them.

No one learned anything useful from that moment. The work didn't improve. The only thing that changed was the sense of safety in the room.

Shame is not feedback. It shuts people down instead of helping them improve.

What You Can Say

When hostility is directed at you:
"I'm open to feedback. I'm not okay with being spoken to that way."

When someone tries to shame you publicly:
"I'll discuss performance one-on-one. This isn't the right forum."

When gossip pulls you in:
"I'm not part of this conversation."

Handling It in Real Time

When someone snaps at you:
"I'll respond once we're both speaking respectfully."

When a coworker is targeted:
"Let's move to solutions. This isn't helping."

When you're blamed unfairly:
"Here's what I completed and when. Let's look at the facts together."

5. Workload Abuse & Burnout Culture

Some workplaces don't have staffing problems, they have a problem with boundaries.

How It Shows Up

- workload that never levels out
- punishment for taking breaks
- urgency culture
- praise only when you sacrifice yourself
- chronic understaffing treated as normal
- high performers given more work instead of relief

A Story You'll Recognize

Think about the person who was always available. Every request was urgent. Every deadline mattered. Saying no wasn't an option because everything was framed as critical. Nights, weekends, vacations, work always came first.

Then a health crisis forced a stop.

When the worker returned months later, something became painfully clear. The same "urgent" work was still sitting there. Unfinished. Unaddressed. Nothing had burned down. Nothing catastrophic had happened. The system had simply waited.

That's when the realization hit: the urgency had never been real. The pressure had existed because they kept taking it.

Workload abuse often hides behind praise. "We knew you could handle it." "We trust you." "You're the one we rely on." But being relied on without relief isn't recognition. It's exploitation.

What You Can Say

When too much lands on your plate:
"Here's everything currently on my list. Which priority should shift to make room for this?"

When they expect two jobs from one person:
"Given my current workload, I'll need direction on what can wait so I can take this on."

When burnout is seen as commitment:
"I care about the quality of my work, and I can't keep up this pace long-term."

Handling It in Real Time

When workload keeps growing:
"Let's list what I can realistically complete today and what needs to move or be reassigned."

When deadlines pile up:
"What's the true priority so I don't split my focus?"

When they refuse to hear "no":
"I can't take this on without something else coming off my plate."

Reflect & Reset

You've just walked through five common ways toxicity shows up at work:

- manipulation disguised as policy
- control and power plays
- favoritism and uneven consequences
- hostility, bullying, and public shaming

- workload abuse and burnout culture

Some of it may have felt familiar. Some of it may have been uncomfortable. You don't need to hold every detail or label everything perfectly right now.

Think back to the moments in this chapter that made you pause. The examples that felt uncomfortably familiar. The sections where you thought, *"That happens here,"* or *"That's why I feel this way."*

Now ask yourself:

- Which of these shows up most often where I work?
- Which one do I find myself brushing off or normalizing because "that's just how it is here"?
- Which situation makes my stress spike the fastest?
- If nothing changed, which of these would wear me down the most over time?
- What is one boundary I could set that would protect me right now?

You don't need a perfect answer. You just need an honest one.

Seeing the pattern clearly is how you stop blaming yourself for it, and start deciding what you need next.

Quick Win - Try This Today

You don't need to fix everything at once. Pick one small boundary that directly interrupts the pattern that's draining you most.

- If your workplace uses guilt, pressure, or "team player" language, leave on time once this week without explaining or apologizing.
- If control or surveillance is constant, stop responding immediately to non-urgent messages and only reply during normal working hours.
- If burnout is treated as commitment, take your full break, even if no one else does.
- If expectations keep shifting, say, *"I'll need to get back to you,"* instead of agreeing on the spot.
- If workload abuse is common, stick to your actual job description for one task and let the overflow stay visible.

Just setting one boundary is a signal to yourself that this stops here.

It protects your peace and gives you space to evaluate what comes next.

When It Doesn't Work

Sometimes you do everything right. You stay calm. You communicate clearly. You set boundaries. You ask for expectations in writing, and the system still doesn't shift. That does not mean you failed.

Here's how to protect yourself:

- document conversations, requests, and shifting expectations
- keep copies of your accomplishments
- identify safe people who support you
- maintain boundaries even when others don't
- involve HR if behavior crosses lines
- if there is no HR, identify the next formal resource
- stop taking responsibility for cultural problems you didn't create

You cannot fix a toxic system alone, but you can refuse to let it cost you more than it already has.

Reality Check

Toxic workplaces don't just hurt productivity. They hurt people.

If you've stayed because you had to, whether for your family, your health, or your stability, that doesn't make you weak. It makes you resilient. You made decisions based on reality, not ideals.

Remember this:

Being treated unfairly does not mean you deserved it.
Being overlooked does not mean you're unskilled.

Being controlled does not mean you're incapable.
Being bullied does not mean you're fragile.

You are surviving an environment that was not built with your well-being in mind. You're still here. Still trying. Still showing up.

Surviving, however, does not mean you have to continue to absorb the damage.

You may not be able to change a toxic system, but you can refuse to let it take more from you. You can stop taking it home. You can stop replaying it in your head. You can decide what you will tolerate and what you will no longer accept.

Seeing the problem clearly makes it possible to act. That might mean setting firmer boundaries, documenting what's happening, speaking up when it's safe, or making a plan for what comes next. What it should not mean is letting the situation continue unchecked just because it's familiar.

You deserve better than toxicity. You deserve room to breathe, respect, safety, and work that doesn't slowly take pieces of you with it.

Until you get there, this chapter helps you hold your ground.

You are not the problem, and you are not alone.

Chapter 13

So You're Ready for What's Next

How to carry what you've learned forward without losing yourself

There comes a point where survival turns into readiness. Not the dramatic kind. Not the "burn it all down" kind. It's quieter than that. It's the realization that something inside you has shifted.

You've learned how to spot unhealthy patterns. You've practiced boundaries, even when it was uncomfortable. You've stopped taking everything personally. You stayed when you had to, and you protected yourself where you could.

Now, you're starting to think beyond just getting through the day. Not because everything is suddenly fixed, but because you are steadier than you were.

This chapter isn't about rushing you out the door. It's about helping you move forward on your terms. Whether that means repositioning yourself where you are, preparing quietly for something new, or simply reclaiming the confidence that the last experience tried to take from you.

A Moment You'll Recognize

There's a moment when you realize you're done trying *here*.

Not angry. Not explosive. Just clear.

You've already done the things people tell you to do. You asked for the raise. You set boundaries and actually held them. You stopped overextending yourself. You documented your work. You waited. You gave it time.

Then someone new gets hired.

They're paid more than you, and their supposed to help, but none of the work ever comes off your plate.

No one says it out loud, but the message lands anyway: things will not change here.

That's when something shifts. You don't vent. You don't announce anything. You just stop trying to make this place work for you.

You update your résumé quietly. You apply selectively. You interview on your lunch break or after hours. You answer questions carefully, without oversharing. You keep doing your job, professionally and steadily, while you prepare.

Eventually, you get an offer. Then a start date.

When you turn in your notice, leadership is surprised. They offer more money. They promise things will be different. Suddenly, there's urgency where there never was before.

But you're not confused anymore.

They had their chance.

You're not leaving out of spite. You're leaving with dignity. You're not running away from something. You're moving toward something that fits better than what you've been holding together.

That's not giving up.

That's moving on with intention.

Before You Move Forward, Take Inventory

When people start thinking about what's next, they often jump straight to job titles, résumés, or applications. That makes sense. It feels productive. But if you skip past this part too quickly, you miss the most important information you have.

That information isn't your job title or how long you stayed.

It's what this experience taught you about how you work, what you can handle, and what you won't accept again.

Before you update anything or apply anywhere, pause and take stock of what you've already lived through.

Not in a "what should I have done differently" way. In a *what did this job actually teach me* way.

Ask yourself questions people really think when they're quietly done trying to make something work:

- What kinds of days did I handle that required judgment, restraint, or leadership even if no one ever called it that?
- Where did I learn my limits the hard way, by staying too long or carrying too much?
- What environments bring out my best work, and which ones slowly wear me down?
- What have I been normalizing simply because it was familiar, not because it was healthy?

This is the information you use to make better decisions next time. It's how you avoid walking into the same role with a different title. It's how you recognize red flags earlier, ask better questions, and choose environments that don't slowly drain you.

This isn't about rewriting the past or regretting how long you stayed. It's about pulling value out of an experience that asked a lot of you.

Nothing you went through was wasted, even if it was never acknowledged or rewarded.

Translating Real Work Into Real Language

One of the hardest parts of moving forward is realizing how much of what you do doesn't *sound* impressive on paper, even though it required skill, judgment, and resilience.

You didn't "just help out."

- You stabilized chaos.
- You filled gaps.
- You trained others.
- You de-escalated situations no one else wanted to handle.
- You prevented problems no one ever saw.

Part of being ready for what's next is learning to describe your work without minimizing it. That means translating reality into language that reflects impact, not ego.

For example:

"I helped when needed" becomes
I supported cross-functional work during staffing gaps to maintain continuity.

"I handled a lot" becomes
I managed competing priorities while maintaining accuracy under pressure.

This isn't an exaggeration. It's a translation.

This matters whether you're updating a résumé, preparing for an internal move, or simply reminding yourself what you're capable of when doubt creeps in.

Using Tools (Including AI) as Support, Not Pressure

You don't have to do this part alone.

If tools like AI feel intimidating or unfamiliar, this is one place they can genuinely help without replacing your voice or experience. You can use these tools to find words for what you already know but have trouble expressing.

Here are some things you can try:

- "Help me describe this responsibility in professional terms."
- "Rewrite this task to reflect problem-solving or leadership."
- "Turn these notes into résumé bullets."
- "Help me practice answering an interview question about conflict or change."

You're still the source. The tool just helps you organize what you already know.

Used this way, it doesn't invent your value. It helps you articulate it.

Preparing Without Broadcasting

You don't have to announce anything to move forward. You're allowed to prepare quietly.

That's often what moving on actually looks like at first. Not big declarations or dramatic exits, but small, steady steps that belong only to you.

It might mean updating your résumé without applying anywhere yet, just to see your experience clearly on the page. It might mean saving examples of work you're proud of, or writing down moments that required judgment, leadership, or restraint, even if no one called them that at the time. It might mean practicing how you'd explain a difficult situation without oversharing, or strengthening relationships with people who genuinely see your value. Sometimes it's simply exploring what else exists, without committing to anything or rushing yourself.

None of this is disloyal. It's self-respect.

You don't owe a workplace your future just because you survived your past there.

One important, grounded reminder belongs here:

Don't quit or give notice until you have a confirmed offer and a start date, unless your situation is unsafe. Always use your best judgment for your situation.

Moving carefully isn't fear. It's financial, emotional, and professional protection. You've worked too hard to put yourself at risk just to prove a point. Thoughtful exits protect the progress you've already made.

If You're Staying, Stay Differently

Sometimes "what's next" still happens in the same place.

Choosing to stay, at least for now, doesn't mean nothing changes, and it doesn't mean you failed to follow through or lacked the courage to leave. Often, it simply means you're making the most responsible decision with the information and resources you have right now.

Staying can be an intentional choice.

When you stay, the shift is internal before it's external. You stop trying to fix what isn't yours to fix. You stop pouring emotional energy into systems that have shown you who they are. You become clearer about your boundaries and more selective about where you invest your effort.

You may decide to be more visible about your work. Not for validation, but so your contributions aren't quietly absorbed without acknowledgment. You may choose to disengage from unnecessary conflict, office politics, or constant urgency that doesn't actually matter. You may focus on doing your job well, protecting your energy, and letting broken systems feel their own weight instead of carrying it for them.

This isn't checking out.

It's checking *in* with yourself.

You can remain professional without remaining unprotected. You can show up with integrity without sacrificing your well-being. You can stop overextending in places that no longer reciprocate your effort.

Staying does not mean surrendering. It means you're deciding, consciously, how much of yourself the job gets, and how much you keep.

And that awareness stays with you, whether you remain where you are or eventually move on.

When Fear Shows Up

Fear often shows up right here, at the moment you decide to protect yourself.

You start asking questions like:

- What if this is as good as it gets?
- What if I try and fail?
- What if I waited too long?

Those doubts don't appear because you're unprepared. They come from spending time in systems that trained you to second-guess your instincts and minimize what you know.

You don't need to feel fully confident to take your next step. You need to trust what you already understand about yourself, your limits, and what no longer works for you.

Moving forward doesn't require certainty. It requires trusting yourself, and that's something you've been building throughout this entire process.

You're further along than you think, and you're moving with intention now.

Reflect & Reset

Ask yourself:

- What have I learned about myself in the last year?
- What am I proud of surviving, even if no one ever acknowledged it?
- What kind of work would let me breathe again?
- What would "enough" actually look like next?
- What support would I offer someone else in this exact position?

Write what's real. Not what sounds impressive.

This isn't about becoming someone new. It's about choosing what you carry forward.

Quick Win - Try This Today

Take a few minutes and capture evidence, not conclusions.

Write down:

- One thing people consistently rely on you for.
- One situation you handled that would have overwhelmed someone new.
- One responsibility that would cause real disruption if you stopped doing it tomorrow.

That's all.

You don't need to polish it.
You don't need to decide what it means yet.
You're simply making sure your experience doesn't disappear just because you stayed capable and professional.

If those realities don't match how you're supported, recognized, or compensated, that gap matters.

You don't have to act on it today, but you also don't need to keep pretending it isn't there.

Reality Check

You are not behind, and you are not starting from zero. You are carrying experience, judgment, resilience, and perspective that only comes from being tested. If you're still standing after everything you navigated, that doesn't make you weak. It means you're capable.

What comes next doesn't have to be perfect, fast, or look like anyone else's path. You don't owe a workplace your future just because you endured it, and you don't have to keep absorbing damage simply because it's familiar. What you went through didn't lower your ceiling. It taught you where your line is.

You're not stuck. You're deciding. When you make your move, it will be intentional, careful, and yours.

The Employee Survival Toolbox

By now, you may have noticed something important.

This book doesn't ask you to overhaul your personality, confront everyone at work, or make dramatic changes overnight. Instead, it gives you small, repeatable tools you can use quietly, safely, and on your own terms.

That is intentional.

You don't need to remember every chapter or apply everything at once. What you have now is a toolbox you can return to whenever work starts to feel heavier than it should.

Here's what's inside.

Say This Instead

Throughout the book, you see specific phrases you can use when work puts you in uncomfortable situations: when your workload keeps growing, when expectations aren't clear, when recognition goes missing, or when someone crosses a line without realizing it.

These scripts aren't about confrontation. They're about staying grounded under pressure.

They help you:

- slow the moment down
- make expectations visible
- protect your time without sounding defensive

- keep your professionalism intact

You don't need to memorize them. You just need to know they exist.

When you feel stuck or caught off guard, come back to the chapter that fits the situation and borrow the language that feels safest for you. Sometimes the right words are all it takes to change how a moment unfolds.

Reflect & Reset

The reflection prompts are not there to fix you. They're there to help you notice patterns.

When work feels overwhelming, confusing, or discouraging, it's often because pressure has been building quietly for a long time. The Reflect & Reset sections help you pause long enough to see what's actually happening.

They're designed to help you:

- separate fact from self-blame
- recognize where the problem is structural, not personal
- identify what's within your control and what isn't
- reconnect with your own judgment

You don't need to answer every question. Even one honest response can bring relief and clarity.

Quick Wins

Not every situation needs a big conversation or a long plan.

The Quick Wins are small actions you can take immediately. Whether that is today, this week, or during your next shift, they help you regain a sense of footing.

They're meant to help you:

- feel less stuck
- reduce mental load
- rebuild momentum
- remind yourself that you still have agency

These aren't shortcuts. They're stabilizers. When everything feels heavy, small wins keep you from tipping over.

Career Boosters

Some of the tools in this book are about getting through the day. Others quietly prepare you for what comes next. Found primarily in Chapter 13, these tools help you translate what you've survived, handled, and learned into language that supports your next opportunity, whether that's a new role, a resume update, or a quiet repositioning where you are.

The Career Booster moments help you:

- make your work visible
- translate what you do into language others understand
- protect your reputation while setting limits

- carry your experience forward with confidence

You don't have to be actively job hunting to use them. They work just as well for repositioning yourself where you are, advocating for yourself, or simply remembering the value you bring.

How to Use This Toolbox Going Forward

You don't need to read this book again from cover to cover.

Keep it nearby. Return to the chapter that matches what you're dealing with right now. Borrow a phrase. Reread a reflection. Try one small adjustment.

Work will change. Pressure will come and go. Some seasons will be harder than others.

This toolbox isn't here to make work perfect. It's here to help you stay steady, capable, and grounded, even when the system around you doesn't make that easy.

You are not powerless.
You are not failing.
You are learning how to survive and grow inside the job you already have.

Epilogue
You're Not Alone

If there's one thing this book was never meant to do, it's tell you to "try harder."

You've already been trying.

You've been adapting, absorbing, adjusting, and holding things together in systems that don't always support you properly. If work has felt heavier than it should, that doesn't mean you're broken. It means the system you're operating in is demanding more than it was built to support.

That's not a personal failure.

Throughout this book, you may have recognized moments you didn't have words for before. Patterns you thought were just "how work is." Situations you quietly blamed yourself for. If nothing else, I hope this gave you language, not to fight, but to stand more steadily inside your own experience.

You are not alone in feeling overwhelmed, overlooked, underpaid, overextended, or unheard. These are shared experiences, even when they feel isolating in the moment. Other people are having the same late-night thoughts, the same knot in their stomach before meetings, the same hesitation before speaking up, the same exhaustion from carrying more than their share.

You're not imagining it. And you're not the only one going through it.

This book wasn't written to push you out the door or pressure you into a dramatic change. It was written to help you stay grounded where you are. To protect your confidence, your energy, and your sense of self while you decide what comes next on your terms.

Thriving doesn't always mean leaving.
Sometimes it means learning how to stop disappearing.
Sometimes it means naming what's happening.
Sometimes it means choosing yourself quietly, one conversation at a time.

You don't need to have everything figured out. You don't need a five-year plan. You don't need to become someone else to survive where you are.

You just need to remember this:

You are capable.
You are allowed to have limits.
You are not alone in this.

Whatever you decide next, whether you stay, shift, prepare, or take a breath, you'll be making that choice with more confidence in yourself than you had before.

That matters more than any job title ever will.

About the Author

Courtney Booth writes about work the way most people actually experience it: complicated, demanding, and often harder than it needs to be. Through years of working in and alongside everyday workplaces, she has seen how capable employees were quietly stretched thin, not because they were doing something wrong, but because the systems around them asked more than they could reasonably give.

Her work centers on helping people understand what's happening beneath the surface at work and providing them with the language, tools, and perspective to stay grounded when quitting isn't an option.

Courtney is the creator of *Work Like a Team*, a people-first platform focused on healthier, more human ways of working. She believes every employee deserves to be treated as a person, not a problem to manage or a resource to use up.